Reading Comprehension

Grade 5

Recently, many students have been taught to read using such "no-fail" techniques as sight reading, picture reading, and whole language.

While it is probable that some students responded well to some of these new techniques, it is also likely that many others were unable to learn to read using these alternative methods. It is for these students that the *Basics First* books were created.

The back-to-basics method is tried and true. It provides students with an approach they can use to learn all of the skills needed for a particular subject. Many of these fundamental techniques may even have helped you learn to read when you were a child!

To help students learn to comprehend what they read, this *Basics First* book offers an interesting fact- or fiction-based story on every other page. Each narrative has been written so that a student at a fifth-grade level can read it successfully. After each story, there are activities that will help students practice the following skills: locating the main idea, reading for details, putting events in order, following directions, determining the cause and the effect of an action, recognizing similarities and differences, analyzing characters, predicting outcomes, drawing inferences, and much more. The carefully thought-out questions help students learn to think, respond, create, imagine, and even do research to learn more about a subject.

You will be thrilled when the students using this book want to read more as they begin to better understand what they are reading. They will also learn to question and will develop higher-level thinking skills that are necessary in so many important aspects in life. Most of all, this book will help students recognize reading as an enjoyable way to spend their time.

Name _____

Emily and David were always competing. Ever since kindergarten, they had competed in sports, grades, and friends. Now they were in fifth grade together and their natural rivalry was about to take off again.

"Watch out for Ms. Dawes," warned Linnette. "She's really angry." Ms. Dawes, their teacher, was furious. Someone had broken her well-deserved "Teacher of the Year" plaque, which was found smashed in the trash. She was offering a ten-dollar reward for information about who did it. David and Emily looked at each other. They were ready for the competition.

"Bet I can solve this mystery before you can," Emily challenged David.

"Don't make me laugh!" answered David in a determined voice.

"They're off!" yelled their friend Daniel when he saw them look at each other.

"I'll bring the criminal to justice!" declared Emily.

"I'll give half of my reward money to anyone who gives me information leading to the capture, arrest, and conviction of the perpetrator," vowed David.

"You two have been watching too much TV," grinned Daniel.

At recess, both kids snooped around for information. After the bell rang, David was still snooping, this time around Ms. Dawes' desk.

"Away from the desk!" Ms. Dawes said. She didn't like anyone to touch it.

"You mean the black hole?" he smirked. Ms. Dawes always had piles of papers, books, and stuff on the desk. She hadn't seen the desktop for months.

"Very funny," she laughed. "I know where everything is, young man. If anyone touches it, they could upset the order. Oh, there are crumbs on my chair. Has someone been eating snacks here?"

Daniel stood in front of the chair. He walked in front of the desk. He went back to the chair. He said, "Hmmm," a few times. He made sure he had their attention.

David and Emily, who were annoyed to be taken away from their investigation, stood with their arms folded in front of them. Emily was tapping her foot.

Suddenly, Daniel declared in a dramatic tone, "I claim the reward in the name of…none other than…me!"

"You?" David and Emily yelled together. "Impossible! How?"

"Elementary, my dear elementary students," Daniel crowed. "These aren't crumbs on Ms. Dawes' chair. They're bits of glass. There was no room for the plaque on her desk, so she put it on the chair. She sat on it. You broke your own plaque, Ms. Dawes. The custodian must have found it and threw it out."

Ms. Dawes was a bit embarrassed, but she did give Daniel the reward. She muttered to herself, "I must clean this desk one of these days."

"Maybe we should work together from now on," suggested Emily to Daniel.

"Three heads are better than one," said David.

"Four are better still," chuckled Linnette.

"I'll think it over," agreed Daniel. "And I'll let you know when the next case comes up!"

Mystery at Snodgrass School

Name _____

Understanding and Enjoying What You Read

Answer the questions below. Reread the story if necessary.

1. Put a check next to the main idea of the story.

   _____ Daniel is smarter than his friends.   _____ A teacher's desk is a mess.

   _____ Kids decide to solve a case.   _____ Offering a reward brings a criminal to justice.

2. Write three words that might describe how David and Emily feel about their competition.

   _____   _____   _____

3. What might David and Emily say to each other about Daniel? _____
   _____

4. What could David and Emily have done to win? _____

5. Why might cooperation sometimes be better than competition? _____
   _____

6. Number the events below in the order in which they occurred.

   _____ Ms. Dawes was angry.   _____ Daniel solved the mystery.

   _____ Ms. Dawes was embarrassed.   _____ Emily knew she'd win.

7. Do you think Daniel is a good detective? Why or why not? _____
   _____

8. What does Daniel mean by "elementary?" Look up this word and write the definition.
   _____

9. Think of the nicest teacher you know and write why you think he or she should be "Teacher of the Year." _____
   _____

10. What is a "black hole?" Why do the kids compare Ms. Dawes' desk to one? _____
    _____

11. On the back of this page, draw a picture of Daniel and his friends next to Ms. Dawes' desk. Remember how the desk is described in the story.

12. Body language, how you place hands and feet or how you look at people, gives people a message. How were David and Emily feeling when they folded their arms while Daniel was getting everybody's attention? _____

    What else did they do that showed they were feeling something while Daniel was talking?
    _____

13. Write a different title for the story. _____

14. What would make you think that there might be more cases for the kids to solve?
    _____

Try This!   Write three things you say that you picked up from a TV show or commercial.

FS-30024 Reading Comprehension

Getting Even With Daniel

Name _____

Emily and David were really irritated by Daniel's attitude since he had cracked The Case of the Broken Plaque, as they called it.

"Let's get even," said Emily. "I read lots of ways to get revenge in that book I borrowed from you."

"Borrowed?" said David. "That was months ago. You're always borrowing my books. I think you're too cheap to buy your own. Well, never mind for now. We'll make up a bogus case for him to solve. Then he'll look dumb when we reveal it's not a real case." The rivals were now united in their revenge.

"What kind of phony case can you dream up?" asked Emily.

"Me?" answered David with surprise. "How about you thinking up something? I do all the work around here."

"Okay, stop complaining. I have the perfect idea. Leave it to me," Emily told him.

"Oh Daniel," called Emily. "Can you help me?" Daniel, who sort of liked Emily, ran right over.

"What can I do for you?" he asked sincerely.

"Daniel, my book money is missing and now I can't order books. I'm sure somebody took it. You're such a good detective, won't you help me?" she looked at him sadly.

"Don't worry, I'll get on the case," he promised, as he rushed away.

Emily felt a little guilty. After all, Daniel was supposed to be her friend. But, he had been so smug about the plaque thing. He deserved a little comeuppance.

Daniel was looking all over and asking questions about the money. He was getting nowhere and was also starting to be a pest. Kids were starting to avoid him.

Two days later, he said to Emily. "I solved the case. Here's your book money."

"My what?" asked Emily. David was too stunned to say anything.

"Your nine dollars and forty-five cents," Daniel announced.

"M-m-m-y what?" Emily repeated as Daniel pressed the money into her hand.

"Don't mention it," said Daniel, and he began to leave. Emily ran after him.

"Uh, Daniel, April Fool!" she said brightly.

"It's December. What's going on?" Daniel asked.

"It was a joke," said Emily, trying to conjure up a smile. "We tricked you."

"Actually, the trick was on you," said Daniel. "I just found that money in the grass. You could have had it." He grabbed the money.

"You never did tell me how much was missing," he said. "That made me suspicious. I decided to test you. At least you didn't keep it."

"I really feel bad, Daniel," Emily said, her head down and her face red.

David came over. "This has gone too far. Can't we all be friends again?"

"I'll let you know," said Daniel. "By the way, I knew it wasn't true. Emily never buys books, she just borrows everybody else's. She's kind of stingy."

The kids decided to make a pact. They would work together, Daniel wouldn't be such a show off, David wouldn't tease Emily about being cheap, and Emily would return things that she borrowed from people.

4

Getting Even With Daniel

Name _____

Understanding and Enjoying What You Read

Answer the questions below. Reread the story if necessary.

1. Put a check next to the main idea of the story.

    _____ Revenge is sweet.   _____ Daniel tricks Emily.

    _____ Emily and David try to trick Daniel.   _____ Emily is cheap.

2. What could Emily have done instead of confessing the trick to Daniel? _____

    _____

3. Why do you think Emily felt guilty? _____

    _____

4. Who would you like for a friend, Daniel, Emily, or David? Why? _____

    _____

5. Are the following statements true or false? Write **T** or **F** next to each one.

    a. _____ Emily knows Daniel likes her.   c. _____ Daniel thought of a scheme.

    b. _____ David felt guilty.   d. _____ Daniel was a good detective.

6. Match the words with the closest meaning by writing a number next to it.

    1. conjure   2. trick   3. pact   4. revenge   5. united   6. comeuppance

    7. stun   8. reveal   9. phony   10. stingy   11. sincerely

    ____ imagine   ____ an agreement   ____ to fool   ____ not generous

    ____ combined; as one   ____ a penalty   ____ fake   ____ getting even

    ____ shock   ____ to make known   ____ honestly

7. Circle all the interrogative sentences in the story. An interrogative sentence asks a question.

8. Why did Emily's face turn red? _____

9. If you were going to be a detective, what equipment would you need? On the back of this page, make a sign advertising your services.

10. Why did Emily say "April Fool" to Daniel? What was she trying to do? _____

    _____

    _____

11. Why were people avoiding Daniel? Why would you avoid someone in your class? _____

    _____

Try This! Write about a time you wanted revenge against someone. Did you do anything about it? What happened? If you didn't do anything about it, why didn't you?

Mistaken Identity

Name _____

Lance was the smallest kid in the class. It was easy to miss him. He was new at school and having a hard time making friends. Some kids picked on him because of his size. He also was becoming known as someone who said he could do just about everything. But most of the time, he got in trouble for doing things wrong. The kids and the teacher were wondering if they could believe Lance. One day, he asked Emily, "Did you know I have a twin brother in room 22?" Emily was surprised. "I thought I knew just about everybody in that room. I don't remember seeing another you," she said.

Lance laughed. "Well, you missed Bob. We look just like two peas in a pod, my dad says. We're exactly alike—identical twins."

"Well, I've never seen peas in a pod, just in a can," said Emily. "But I'll watch out for him." At recess, Emily waited to see who came out of the room next door. Nobody looked like Lance. When the bell rang, Lance stood next to Emily. He pointed at someone.

"There's Bob," he said as he pointed out a boy who was four inches taller and ten pounds heavier than he, and who had a wide face and freckles. Emily yelled to him, "Are you Lance's twin brother?" He grinned and yelled back, "I sure am, although I'm surprised you can tell us apart. We're like two peas..."

"In a pod," Emily finished for him.

"They always put us in separate classes because we play tricks on the teacher," he laughed. "Sometimes we even fool our parents."

Emily looked and looked. They both had freckles. However, that was about the only way they looked alike. She whispered to David, "Am I crazy? Do they really look alike?"

David shook his head. "They sure don't. This sounds like another Lance trick to get attention. Hey, I have an idea. Let's teach him a lesson."

The next day, Emily went up to Lance. "Hi, Bob," she smiled.

"I'm Lance," he said. Emily laughed. "Sure you are. Quit joking."

"Hey, Bob, you're in the wrong line. The teacher's going to get mad," said David.

Soon everybody was teasing him. Lance didn't know what was going on.

"I'm Lance!" he insisted. This went on all day. Soon, Bob was also telling people that the two of them were twins. Before school was over, Lance asked Ms. Dawes if he could say something in front of the class. The teacher agreed.

"I give up! I'm Lance! This has happened to me all my life! Everybody mixes up my brother and me because we're identical twins! From now on, I'm going to wear green, and he'll wear blue. Or maybe I'll wear blue, and he'll wear green. Or maybe…Well, I don't know, but there will be no more mix-ups." Lance was really serious!

David and Emily looked at each other. Lance and Bob really were twins!

The next day, Lance and Bob surprised the kids again. Lance was wearing a T-shirt that said, *I'm not him, I'm Lance.* Bob's said, of course, *I'm not him, I'm Bob.* Emily said, "Well, I don't know why they think they look alike, but I'll go along with it." She called out to Lance, "Big improvement, Lance. We'll never get you and Bob mixed-up again."

⟨6⟩

Mistaken Identity

Name _____

Understanding and Enjoying What You Read

Answer the questions below. Reread the story if necessary.

1. Put a check next to the main idea of the story.

    _____ A boy and his twin brother go to school together.

    _____ Emily and David play a trick on Lance.

    _____ Lance and Bob are identical twins who don't look alike.

    _____ Lance tricks his classmates.

2. How would you change the ending to this story? _____
    _____

3. Why do you think Lance wants everyone to believe that he and his twin brother look alike?
    _____

4. Number the events below in order.

    _____ Lance insists he and Bob are twins.

    _____ Lance talks to the class.

    _____ Emily sees Bob for the first time.

    _____ Lance is the smallest kid in the class.

    _____ Lance decides that he and his brother should wear different colors each day.

5. What else do you think looks like "two peas in a pod?"_____

6. Do you think Lance really believes he and his brother look alike? Explain. _____
    _____

7. On the back of this paper, draw a picture of someone who would look just like you.

8. What would you do if you had a twin? Would you dress alike? Would you try to fool people? If so, how? _____
    _____

9. What did you think would happen when the kids pretended that Lance was Bob? _____
    _____

10. How do you think Bob and Lance should make sure they're not mistaken for each other? _____
    _____

11. What are the differences between Lance and Bob? How does each look?
    Bob _____   Lance _____

12. What could Lance do so the kids won't pick on him anymore? _____
    _____

13. Write antonyms (words that are opposites) for the words below.

    wide _____   apart _____   friends _____   wrong _____

14. Underline the contractions in the story.

Try This!

Draw a picture of what you think Lance and Bob look like. Write a scene depicting the two of them talking together.

FS-30024 Reading Comprehension

Name _____

"It's my birthday on Tuesday!" shouted Emily. "I'm so excited. Everybody will be able to celebrate. My mother will bring cookies for the whole class."

David shrugged his shoulders. "Well, it's George Washington's birthday too, and Ms. Dawes said we're going to have a party for him. We'll have cherry pie and old-fashioned food like johnnycakes—yuck! Whatever that is, I know I won't like it. So, nobody's going to even notice your birthday!"

Emily realized he was right! She thought about it all day. Ms. Dawes had to remind her to pay attention several times during science. She was so distracted that she messed up her group's experiment. After school, she got home and stomped into the living room.

"Mom, it's not fair!" she grumbled. "Why do I have to share my birthday with George Washington? Nobody is going to pay any attention to me at school."

Emily's mom sighed. "Sometimes, Emily, you're very selfish. Me, me, me! You should feel honored to share his birthday."

"Big deal!" shouted Emily. "He didn't even really chop down that stupid cherry tree. And he had wooden teeth! Gross!"

"Sit down," said her mom. "I'll tell you a few more things about Washington."

"Do I have to?" Emily asked, but Mom was pointing to the sofa.

"Well, history always stretches the truth about heroes, but George really was one. He didn't just send his men off to war. He went along with them, putting himself in danger too. Do you remember that picture of him crossing the Delaware? He really did. Of course, he probably wasn't silly enough to stand up in the boat the whole time. When he was younger, he had had an illness called smallpox. It left big holes, kind of like chickenpox, only bigger, all over his face."

"Oh, no, I share a birthday with an ugly guy!"

"Listen!" said Mom. "In his day, lots of people got smallpox. They would fill the holes on their faces with warm, soft wax, which would harden. Then they'd cover their faces with white powder, kind of like makeup. When they'd go to parties, they couldn't stand too close to fireplaces."

"Their faces would melt!" yelled Emily. "Poor George! I don't think he'd mind if I called him by his first name. After all, we share a birthday! Imagine, he still became president, and married Martha! If he went to our school, everybody would laugh at him!"

"Well," said Mom, "that wasn't exactly my point, but…"

"I wish he could come back," sighed Emily. "He could have plastic surgery. I'd just die if I looked like that! I'll share my birthday with the poor man. And I won't tell anybody the way he really looked."

"Chocolate chip or snickerdoodles?" asked Mom, shaking her head.

"Instead of cookies," Emily thought out loud, "how about cherry pie in honor of my friend George? And, suppose we give our bird a new name? Let's call her Georgina! I think I'll tell Ms. Dawes that I'll do an extra credit report on the real George Washington. What else can I do?" Emily asked no one in particular.

8

Happy Birthday to Us!

Name _____

Understanding and Enjoying What You Read

Answer the questions below. Reread the story if necessary.

1. Put a check next to the main idea of the story.
   - _____ Emily is worried about sharing her birthday.
   - _____ George Washington had smallpox.
   - _____ It's a privilege to share a birthday with a president.
   - _____ Washington had wooden teeth.

2. Write two facts you know about George Washington. _____
   _____
   _____

3. Write **T** or **F** to show whether each sentence is true or false.
   - _____ George Washington didn't want to share his birthday with Emily.
   - _____ Emily's mom was going to make cookies for her birthday.
   - _____ Emily was related to George Washington.
   - _____ George married Martha.
   - _____ George had smallpox.

4. With whom would you like to share your birthday? Why? _____
   _____

5. What kind of person is Emily's mom? _____

6. If George Washington didn't truly chop down a cherry tree when he was a boy, why do you think that story is told? _____

7. Why does Emily's mom think her daughter is selfish? _____
   _____

8. What is your favorite kind of cookie? Why do you like it? _____
   _____

9. What do you think might be in a dish called "johnnycake?" _____
   _____

10. In your own words, write what people who had smallpox scars used to do. _____
    _____

11. David knows he won't like johnnycakes even before tasting them. What does that tell you about his character? _____

12. Draw a rectangle around all the present participles, or words that end in *-ing*.

13. If George Washington came back today, what would you want him to see that he couldn't have seen in his day? _____

14. Why did Mom think Emily was overdoing it? _____

Try This!

Write a list of questions you would like to ask George Washington if you met him.

FS-30024 Reading Comprehension

Name _____

Ms. Dawes' students at Snodgrass Elementary school were so excited! Five students would be chosen to appear on KidGames, the game show for kids.

"Students," Ms. Dawes began, "now I don't want anyone to feel bad. You were chosen at random, and the winners are…" she paused, "Emily, David, Daniel, Miguel, and Linnette." Disappointment could be heard throughout the class.

"Don't mess up!" shouted those who were not chosen to be the lucky winners.

The lucky kids went to the city by bus. "I have butterflies in my stomach," said Emily. "Butterflies!" said David. "I have elephants!" All five kids agreed they were nervous.

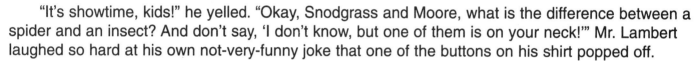

"'Now, remember," said Ms. Dawes, "you have to keep your heads and beat the team from Moore School." They knew that Ms. Dawes had her own competition with Mr. Frewer, a teacher at Moore, the school that had won three years in a row.

The kids entered the studio, and everyone sat down. The master of ceremonies was Richard Lambert who jumped around and smiled a lot with what looked like about a million teeth.

"It's showtime, kids!" he yelled. "Okay, Snodgrass and Moore, what is the difference between a spider and an insect? And don't say, 'I don't know, but one of them is on your neck!'" Mr. Lambert laughed so hard at his own not-very-funny joke that one of the buttons on his shirt popped off.

Quick as a wink, Moore's buzzer went off, and Monica Netro answered, "Spiders, which are arachnids, have eight legs. Insects have six." The points went up on the scoreboard. Soon, Moore and Snodgrass were neck and neck.

Daniel whispered to Emily, "We're going to lose! Nobody can beat them. And Linnette is tongue-tied. We need her for science questions!"

"This is the tie-breaker, kiddies," said the obnoxious host. "Snodgrass, this is your last chance. Maybe your robot knows something." They looked at poor Linnette. That was mean, thought Emily.

"When did Albert Einstein die and how old was he?" asked Lambert. I have to do something, thought Emily. She stepped on Linnette's foot, really hard. Linnette came out of her trance with a start.

"Albert Einstein, 1879-1955, one of the greatest scientists of all time. He died at age 76."

"That's right! Snodgrass wins!" shouted Lambert. The team cheered. Ms. Dawes hugged them all. They shook hands with the Moore team, all except Linnette, who was still reciting, "He is best known for his theory of relativity, $E=mc^2$, which he advanced at age 26. He made many other contributions to science, like helping the United States build the first atomic bomb. He was offered the presidency of the young nation of Israel, but refused. When he was a child, Einstein showed no early signs of genius. He was an immigrant from Germany to the United States and settled in Princeton, New Jersey. He was…"

The team picked her up and carried her to the bus. About halfway back to school, she came out of her trance. "Did we win?" she asked. Ms. Dawes thrust the trophy into Linnette's arms.

FS-30024 Reading Comprehension

Name _____

Understanding and Enjoying What You Read
Answer the questions below. Reread the story if necessary.

1. The main idea of this story is:

_____ Albert Einstein was a great scientist.

_____ The class went on a game show to win a trophy.

_____ Ms. Dawes had a rivalry with another teacher.

_____ Snodgrass won a trophy.

_____ Linnette won the game for them.

2. Answer the questions.

Who knew a lot about Einstein?_____

For what is Einstein famous?_____

How did Einstein help the United States? _____

3. Why do you think Linnette knew so much about Einstein? _____

_____

4. How old would Einstein be if he were alive today? _____

5. Why might Linnette have been in a trance? What is a trance? _____

_____

6. What kind of person was the host?_____

7. Pretend you are the host of a game show. Write what you would say to make people feel
welcome and comfortable on your show. _____

_____

_____

8. On the back of this page, write the rules for a game show that you invent. Write five questions
and answers and try them on a friend, family member, or classmate.

9. Mr. Lambert's joke wasn't very funny. Write a funny joke that you know. _____

_____

_____

10. Write the correct word from the box for each sentence.

a. Her friend talked a lot and wanted everyone's attention. He was _____ .

b. He stopped what he was doing and _____ for a moment.

c. None of Einstein's teachers thought he was a _____ .

d. Einstein made many contributions to _____.

| genius |
| science |
| paused |
| obnoxious |

Try This! Plan a game show with a few of your friends. Make up some questions and
answers and try them on your friends.

The Dark and Stormy Night

Name _____

"I love reading these *Fright Night* books," said David, as he put down his book. He continued, "This one was about a girl who got locked in a basement accidentally, and this other girl who looks really weird comes down and Francie, that's the girl locked in the basement, sees that she can see right through the other girl, and…"

"Too scary for me," said Daniel. "I don't want to hear any more!"

"Me, too," agreed Emily. "I don't like being terrified or frightened."

"Oh, I don't know," said Linnette, "I like the feeling I get from a good scare."

"Then you wouldn't mind going to my new house," grinned Emily. "We just bought the Perkins place at the edge of town. I want to see my new room and decide what color I want it to be painted. What do you think of peach?"

"I think your family must be crazy!" said Daniel. "Spooky old man Perkins died in that house years ago. Nobody has been in it for years. What was wrong with your old house?"

"Nothing," said Emily, "but this one is much bigger and has a huge yard all my pets can run around in." Emily adopted every stray animal in town. She had rabbits, dogs, cats, birds, and even a squirrel that came in the house for treats.

"Okay, I'll go," each one agreed in turn. They couldn't let Emily go alone, even if it was going to be her home.

The friends met and rode their bikes to the old Perkins house after dinner. It didn't look so bad in the twilight. Suddenly, it began to rain, then thunder and lightning crashed through the sky, which quickly turned it dark.

"Oh, no!" said Daniel. "It's a dark and stormy night! Something awful is going to happen. And I just thought of something else! It's Friday the thirteenth."

The kids turned their bikes around and began to leave, but a tree fell and blocked their exit. "We'll just have to go into the house," said Emily. The kids got off their bikes and followed her as if they were going to their doom. She opened the door, and it creaked. They heard someone walking towards them. The kids looked for a place to hide, but it was too dark. "Ouch!" said Linnette as she bumped into a piece of wood. The kids began to scream.

"What's going on?" asked a voice. The lights went on. The house was warm and cozy and filled with furniture. The storm seemed far away. The old Perkins house had changed from the neighborhood haunted house into the perfect place for a nice family like Emily's.

"Welcome to our new home," said Emily's dad. "She told us she was bringing you all. I think maybe she didn't tell you we were settled here already. Have some hot chocolate and cookies. It's a dark and stormy night out there. Call your parents and ask if everyone can stay overnight. Tomorrow's Saturday—no school!"

The kids looked around. Emily was lucky. "Come on, I'll give you a tour," Emily said proudly. "This house is full of nooks and crannies and secret places, thanks to Mr. Perkins. We can pick one and tell ghost stories."

"I think we've had enough scary stuff tonight," said Linnette.

"This is more fun than *Fright Night* books," said David. Everyone agreed.

The Dark and Stormy Night

Name _____

Understanding and Enjoying What You Read

Answer the questions below. Reread the story if necessary.

1. Put a check next to the main idea of the story.
   - _____ The friends are afraid of dark and stormy nights.
   - _____ They eat milk and cookies.
   - _____ All the kids love to read scary stories.
   - _____ Emily takes her friends to her new house.
   - _____ The kids run into a storm.

2. Would you move to a scary house? Why or why not? _____
   _____

3. Why do you think people like to read scary stories? _____
   _____

4. What made the tree fall down? _____

5. Number the events in the order in which they occurred.
   - _____ The kids got on their bikes and tried to ride away.
   - _____ Emily's dad had hot chocolate and cookies ready.
   - _____ Emily said her family was moving.
   - _____ Daniel was scared by *Fright Night* books.
   - _____ Emily told her friends about her new house.

6. What is one thing you know about Emily's character from the story? _____

7. Write three words that mean the same as *scary*. _____ _____ _____

8. Why do you think Emily fooled her friends about her house? _____
   _____

9. On the back of this page, draw what the kids expected Emily's house to look like.

10. Write a different ending for the story. _____
    _____

11. What time of day did the kids ride to the old house? _____

12. Why did Daniel think Emily's family was crazy? _____
    _____

13. What do you think of Emily's friends? _____
    _____

14. Why are people afraid of Friday the thirteenth? What could happen on that day? _____

15. Circle the best synonym (word that means the same, or nearly the same) for *doom*.

    scare   death   house   room

Try This!

Write a "dark and stormy night" story.

FS-30024 Reading Comprehension

Name _____

Emily was shopping for her birthday party. "Now let's see," she said aloud. "What did Mom tell me to get? She didn't give me much money. I'd really like to get lots of special stuff for my friends." Just then, Daniel came by.

"Guess you're getting ready for the big party, right? Well, don't forget, I can't eat peanuts. I swell up like a balloon if I eat them."

"Okay, no peanuts," said Emily. "I also can't get chocolate for Linnette, coconut for Brett, and spinach for Bo. Bo didn't have to worry about that one. I'm just going to get everything, and they can figure it out for themselves. Oh, when I came in, they gave out this ticket at the door, and I don't know what it's for. I'll just throw it away. It's probably just an ad."

"Miguel is on a diet, so don't get a lemon cake, because then he'll go off his diet and blame you. And…" Just then, a booming voice came over the loudspeaker.

"Attention, shoppers, those of you with the numbers 451, 555, and 682 are the contestants in our supermarket race. Just bring your carts to the starting line at the front. Whoever's cart adds up to the most money wins his or her basket of groceries!"

Emily looked at her ticket. "Six eight two! That's me! I win!" She dashed up to the front and showed her ticket.

"Where's your mother, little girl?" asked the manager.

"She's picking me up at five o'clock," said Emily. "Here's my number!"

"This is great!" Daniel said. "You can get whatever you need for the party. Then we'll have the best party, and it'll be free!" For once, Emily agreed with him.

"Ready, set, go!" yelled the manager as the three contestants took off down the aisles like they were shot out of a cannon. Daniel yelled encouragement: "Go, go, faster! Get party stuff!" Emily went from the candy department to the paper goods, to the sodas, to the bakery, to pet food. Her basket was filling up, but it didn't look full of expensive stuff. She had an idea. She went to the fancy food section of the market and loaded up with cans and packages of weird stuff she had never heard of but knew was expensive. As Emily rounded the last aisle, heading for the checkout counter, her basket almost tipped over! She used all her strength to set it upright.

"Good save!" screeched Daniel with approval. The bell rang, and Emily raced to the counter where she was checked out. Daniel was waiting for her.

"Miss, you win by forty-two cents. Congratulations!" The other shoppers applauded, then continued with their shopping. The excitement was over.

When Emily's mom came at exactly five o'clock, she was shocked by all the groceries she saw. "You are really a good shopper, Emily," she said. "I didn't think I gave you that much money." Emily told her mom what had happened.

Emily's party was fun. She showed a video, and her guests played games. Brett did magic tricks that worked for the most part. He wanted to saw Linnette in half, but Linnette wouldn't cooperate. The best part was the food. There were lots of pizzas, and nobody knew they were frozen pizzas from the market. There was a yummy cake with no coconut, chocolate, or peanuts. But some of the food made the kids remark, "Isn't the food sort of weird? I mean, lemon grass soup, glazed chestnuts, and yak cheese?" Emily just smiled.

Supermarket Race

Name _____

Understanding and Enjoying What You Read

Answer the questions below. Reread the story if necessary.

1. Put a check next to the main idea of the story.

    ___ Emily buys expensive food.

    ___ Emily gets to be a contestant.

    ___ Emily goes shopping for her birthday party and wins free food.

    ___ Emily wants free food.

2. Why do you think Daniel wants Emily to win? _____

3. Why do you think the food Emily bought was so expensive? _____

    _____

4. Underline every word in the story that has to do with food.

5. If Emily would not have won, what might she have served at the party? _____

    _____

6. Why did the market manager ask for Emily's mother? _____

    _____

7. What were the winning numbers? _____ _____ _____ Circle Emily's.

8. What do you think of Emily's party? Would you like to attend? Why or why not? _____

    _____

9. What departments in the market did Emily visit? _____

10. Name the foods that Emily's friends couldn't eat. _____

11. Name a food that you think is "fancy." _____

12. Retell what happened at Emily's party, in order. _____

    _____

    _____

    _____

13. How do you think Emily's mother felt when she found out Emily had won? _____

    _____

14. Do you think that Brett is a good magician? Explain. Would you let him saw you in half? Why or why not? _____

    _____

15. What is the difference between *aisle* and *isle*? Both sound the same but have different meanings and are spelled differently. Look them up if necessary.

    aisle _____   isle _____

Try This! If you could have anything in the grocery store for free, what would you want? Write as much as you can in three minutes. How much do you think these items would cost?

FS-30024 Reading Comprehension

A Day at the Beach

Name _____

"We sure are lucky to live near the beach," David said to Emily one day as they were soaking up the sun. Daniel came and threw a blanket over them.

"What are you doing?" Emily sputtered as she came out from under the blanket.

"Don't you know that the sun is very bad for you?" he scolded.

"But we want to get a tan. My mother left us here until dinnertime," said Emily.

"The sun's ultraviolet rays are very bad for the human skin, especially when somebody is a redhead like you, freckle face," Daniel teased Emily.

"Freckle face? Take this!" She pushed Daniel down. David came over, and they both started covering Daniel with sand.

"I give up!" he yelled. "But it's not a joke. My Uncle Roy is a doctor, and he said the sun gives people cancer and wrinkles your skin like a prune. And it's going to get worse, because the ozone layer has a hole in it."

"I hear a lot about the ozone layer," said David. "What is it?"

"I know," said Emily, raising her hand as though she was in school. "It's a layer of gas that surrounds Earth. As long as it's there, it protects us from the sun's ultraviolet rays. There are a couple of places over Earth where the ozone has holes. So now, the rays are hitting Earth."

"That's pretty good," said Daniel. "Since you know so much, how come you're broiling out here like a hot dog?"

"It's easy to forget," admitted Emily. "Who thinks about the ozone layer?"

"I don't have to worry, anyway," bragged David. "My skin is a lot darker than Emily's."

"Maybe you don't have to worry as much as Emily, but the sun isn't good for you, either," said Daniel. "See, I have this lotion that protects my skin." He showed it to his friends. "You can use some if you like. And I brought an umbrella." David and Emily put on the lotion. They moved their beach stuff under the umbrella.

"Let's go for a swim," said Emily. "Then we'll sit under your nerdy, I mean necessary, umbrella. Last one in's a doofus!" They ran into the surf, but ran out two seconds later. Daniel was running the fastest.

"Shark! Great white! Call the police! Call the mayor! Call Jacques Cousteau!" yelled Daniel.

"I guess you haven't been to the beach for awhile," said David.

"You mean there are sharks in the water now? I'm glad I don't come here much," said Daniel, shaking. "That's Jaws!"

"That's Jaws, all right. 'Jaws' Johnson. He wears a fin on his back so people won't swim near him." Emily laughed. "He wants to be a sharkologist."

"A sharkologist?" asked David. "Is that a real word?"

"I know that people who study fish are called ichthyologists," said Daniel. "Maybe those who study just sharks are called sharkologists."

"I'll tell you what," said David to Daniel. "You protect us from the sun, and we'll keep you safe from Jaws!" They lay under the umbrella with sunglasses, T-shirts, and hats. "Jaws" joined them later.

A Day at the Beach

Name _____

Understanding and Enjoying What You Read
Answer the questions below. Reread the story if necessary.

1. Put a check next to the main idea of the story.
   ___ Three friends have a fun day at the beach.
   ___ David and Emily learn about sun protection.
   ___ Daniel is frightened by a shark.
   ___ A man pretends to be a shark.
   ___ Emily has red hair.

2. If there really was a shark in the water, what should the kids have done? _____
_____

3. The ozone layer is a thin layer of a gas called ozone that protects our planet from the harmful rays of the sun. What do you think would happen if it disappeared?_____
_____
_____

4. Jacques Cousteau is a Frenchman who explores the oceans. Would you like to do that? Why or why not? _____
_____

5. What kind of person do you think "Jaws" Johnson is? _____
_____

6. When was Emily's mother going to pick her up at the beach? _____

7. What is someone who studies fish called? _____

8. What was David bragging about? _____

9. Why would redheads be more likely to be harmed by the sun's rays? _____
_____

10. On the back of this page, make a list of rules for protecting yourself at the beach.

11. The sun is about 93 million miles away. How can it hurt us from such a distance? _____
_____

12. What would you do if you saw "Jaws" Johnson in the water and you knew it was him? _____
_____

13. Circle all the nouns in the story that have anything to do with the beach.

14. Where do you like to swim? Write about your favorite place. _____
_____
_____

Try This!   Write a story about what you would do on a day at the beach.

FS-30024 Reading Comprehension

The Substitute

Name _____

"Don't look now, but Ms. Dawes is absent, and our substitute is Mrs. Hunter," said David in a somber voice.

"Old Headhunter?" squeaked Emily. "She hates us!"

"She hates everybody! She hates kids!" groaned Daniel.

"She's at least 95 years old! I bet she was Abe Lincoln's substitute!"

"This is going to be the worst day of the year. I should have stayed home," moaned Lance.

"Just because we play tricks on her, she's mean," mentioned Daniel. "You're supposed to make it hard for substitutes. It's what kids do!"

"Even if you get up to sharpen a pencil, she yells at you!" said David.

"She doesn't let you go to the bathroom. Isn't that against the law?"

"Let's do something," suggested Linnette. "Then she won't come back—never, ever again. It'll have to be something good."

The kids in room 21 made their plans. A few minutes later, class began.

"Good morning," said Mrs. Hunter in a very pleasant voice. The kids were surprised.

"Don't be caught off guard," said Emily. "A leopard doesn't change its spots. It said so in that story we read yesterday. One, two, three." Exactly on the count of three, everyone in class dropped their very heavy science books. Thirty-four books made a very loud noise. Everyone looked surprised.

Mrs. Hunter didn't say a word. She dropped her book on the floor, too. Then she wrote something on a piece of paper. She said, "Open your reading books, please, to page 93." The next trick was about to begin.

"Linnette, please read." Emily read instead. "Very nice," said Mrs. Hunter, and she wrote again. "David, please read." Daniel read. There was more writing. She had a seating chart so she knew she was being hoodwinked, but she wasn't getting angry.

"I bet she's writing a note to Ms. Dawes about how bad we are. We're going to be in big trouble. We should cancel the next trick." But it was too late. Everyone began to whistle the song "Whistle While You Work." Mrs. Hunter whistled with them, then wrote some more. She put down the pencil and smiled at the class.

"She smiled!" said Brett. "She never smiles. There's something wrong!"

"No more tricks, pass it on," said Emily. For the rest of the day, the class was really good. Mrs. Hunter was different.

"Maybe she's twins, and this is the nice one," suggested Linnette. If someone talked, Mrs. Hunter would write. When Bo tripped Brett, Mrs. Hunter wrote, then smiled.

"This is too much. I'm cracking up," said Daniel dramatically.

The next day, Ms. Dawes returned. She read Mrs. Hunter's note, frowned and shook her head. Gulps and "Uh, ohs" could be heard throughout the room.

"Do you want to see her note?" she asked. No one said a word. She held it up. On a big piece of paper, Mrs. Hunter had written, GOTCHA! SEE YOU NEXT TIME. REGARDS FROM OLD MRS. HEADHUNTER. P.S. LINCOLN WAS A GOOD BOY!

18

The Substitute

Name _____

Understanding and Enjoying What You Read

Answer the questions below. Reread the story if necessary.

1. Put a check next to the main idea of the story.

    ___ Ms. Dawes reads a note.

    ___ A substitute teaches a class a lesson.

    ___ Mrs. Hunter is a mean teacher.

    ___ The kids played tricks on a substitute.

    ___ Kids don't like a mean substitute.

2. Write what you think "hoodwinked" means. Then look it up in a dictionary and write the definition. _____
   _____

3. What do you think of Mrs. Hunter? What kind of person is she? _____
   _____

4. Write a note for a substitute telling him or her things to know about your class. _____
   _____

5. A noun is a person, place, or thing. Circle all the nouns in this story.

6. Write four words that can take the place of "said" in a quotation. For example: "Open your books," she **said.** _____ _____ _____ _____

7. What did you think Mrs. Hunter would do when the kids began playing tricks? _____
   _____

8. Why do you think Mrs. Hunter changed? _____
   _____

9. Why did Mrs. Hunter seem to be writing so much all day? _____
   _____

10. What did Mrs. Hunter's note mean? _____

11. Why were the kids so mean to Mrs. Hunter? _____
    _____

12. What does Daniel mean when he says he's "cracking up?" _____
    _____

13. If Mrs. Hunter had really been a substitute for Abraham Lincoln, that could have been in about 1820. If she was 20 years old at the time, how old would she be today? _____

14. How many tricks did the class play on Mrs. Hunter? _____

15. Why do you think they call her "Mrs. Headhunter?" _____
    _____

Try This! Write your ideas about who would be the perfect teacher and why.

FS-30024 Reading Comprehension

The Scavenger Hunt

Main idea, grammar, critical thinking, inference, vocabulary, sequencing, character analysis

Name _____

Linnette, Emily, David, Daniel, and their friends were invited to Lance's house for a birthday party. Lance and his twin brother Bob were having their birthday party together. When the friends arrived, Lance was wearing a T-shirt that read, *I'm Lance. I'm the oldest by three minutes.* Bob's T-shirt read, *I'm Bob. We look alike, but I'm the youngest.* The kids just chuckled. Everybody except Lance and Bob knew the twins didn't look like twins. They barely looked like brothers. Lance gave everyone an envelope and told them not to open it.

"What's going on?" asked Linnette. "Where's the cake, ice cream, and stuff?"

"Be patient," grinned Lance mischievously.

"Okay, open your envelopes!" the twins said together.

This was really mysterious. Inside each envelope was a sheet of paper that said, "Scavenger Hunt! In order to get your party foods, favors, and fun, you have to find everything below. You can work in teams of no more than two and may go as far as around the block. Good luck!" The kids yelled with approval. This would be fun!

David and Emily decided to become partners, as did Daniel and Linnette. Here's the list they had: 1. Two leaves from a non-deciduous tree 2. Material a bird might use for a nest 3. Something made of wood 4. A piece of paper with something printed on it 5. Something recyclable 6. A piece of thread 7. Any kind of seed 8. Pet food 9. Something to draw with 10. Something valuable

Everyone scurried about looking for everything on the list. Everybody had a different idea of what was valuable. They asked neighbors for thread. They searched the wastebasket in Lance's house for something with printing on it. They raided his bird's cage for a seed. (Buzzy, his cockatiel, was very angry about that.) Linnette and Daniel knew from science that a deciduous tree was one that loses its leaves in fall. They combed the neighborhood. Some trees had lost their leaves. They were deciduous. They snipped some pine needles from a big tree in front of the house. Pine trees kept their needles practically forever. The one that puzzled them, however, was number 10. David and Emily returned to the party first, after tracking down almost everything.

"We have everything," David smiled. When everyone else returned, Lance and his father checked everything off. It was interesting to see what each team thought was valuable. Linnette and Daniel had found a gold-colored safety pin.

"Well, it looks like gold," they insisted.

Brett and Bo had found a quarter.

"That's not so valuable," said Miguel.

"So what did you find?" Daniel asked him. Miguel proudly showed them a lottery ticket. "This could be a real winner."

"If it was, why would anybody throw it in the street?" asked Brett. Finally, it was David and Emily's turn.

"You're missing something valuable," Lance's dad said. David and Emily patted each other's shoulders and shook their heads.

"No we're not," insisted Emily. "We have the most valuable thing of all—friends. David and me."

"Now why didn't we think of that?" Daniel wondered out loud.

FS-30024 Reading Comprehension

The Scavenger Hunt

Name _____

Understanding and Enjoying What You Read

Answer the questions below. Reread the story if necessary.

1. Put a check next to the main idea of the story.

    ____ David and Emily win a scavenger hunt.   ____ Lance has a party.

    ____ David and Emily find something valuable.   ____ There are ten things to find.

    ____ Kids go to Bob and Lance's birthday party and participate in a scavenger hunt.

2. Number the events in the order in which they occurred.

    ____ David and Emily win.   ____ Linnette and Daniel snip pine needles.

    ____ The kids open their envelopes.   ____ Lance and his father check off the items.

    ____ Lance acts mysterious.

3. Circle all the pronouns in the story. Remember, pronouns are words that refer to people: *I, me, you, he, him, she, her, it, we, us, they, them, my, mine, yours, his, hers, its, ours, theirs.*

4. If you were going on the scavenger hunt in this story, what would you get that you think is valuable? Explain why. _____

5. Why do you think David and Emily were able to find things so quickly? _____

    _____

6. What do you think you know about the kind of person Lance is from this story? _____

    _____

7. What do you think was the prize for winning the scavenger hunt? _____

8. Look at the list from Lance and Bob's party. Write what you would get for each item.

    1. _____   2. _____   3. _____

    4. _____   5. _____   6. _____

    7. _____   8. _____   9. _____

9. What "valuable" things were found? Do you think they were really valuable? Explain._____

    _____

10. What kind of a bird is a cockatiel? Look it up in a dictionary. Then write what kind of bird you would get and why. _____

    _____

    _____

11. Design a T-shirt for yourself that tells, in very few words, something that you'd like people to know about yourself. Draw it on the back of this paper.

12. Write five things about good friends that make them valuable._____

    _____

13. What does "they combed the neighborhood" mean?_____

    _____

Try This!   Write ten things you think your class could find on a scavenger hunt.

FS-30024 Reading Comprehension

Name _____

"I'm not ready for this test," said David. "Ms. Dawes is asking too much stuff."

"I know," agreed Linnette, "geography, spelling, math, and science together."

"I almost didn't come today," said Brett nervously. "I told my mom I had a stomachache. She said I just had testaphobia. That means 'fear of tests.' This test will probably give me a stomachache for real."

"I'm not worried," boasted Daniel. "I've worked out a system to remember lots of different facts. My mom knew some of this when she was in school."

"If it's that old, maybe it's not good anymore." said David.

"Trust me," said Daniel convincingly. "I'll share everything with you."

Throughout lunch, the kids studied Daniel's tips. They memorized, tested each other, wrote notes, and then the bell rang. They tore up the notes, and they were ready. After lunch, Ms. Dawes passed out the papers.

Name the five Great Lakes was the first question. Daniel thought, It spells HOUSES. Huron, Ontario, U..U..U.. no, that couldn't be right. HOMES. That means Huron, Ontario, Michigan, Erie, and Superior. Got it.

"Write the nine planets in our solar system in order," Emily mumbled. Mars, Milky Way, Pluto, Goofy, Venus, Diana—oh no! she thought. I just named candy bars, cartoon characters, and ancient goddesses! Suddenly, a vision of her mother popped into her head. "I got it!" she yelled out loud. Ms. Dawes gave her a stern look.

"I can do this," Emily whispered to herself. She remembered the clue that Daniel had taught them: **M**y **v**ery **e**xcellent **m**other **j**ust **s**at **u**nder **n**ew **p**ines. It didn't make much sense as a sentence, but it made her write Mercury, Venus, Earth, Mars, Jupiter, Saturn, Uranus, Neptune, Pluto. The first letter of each word in the silly sentence was also the first letter of a planet. It worked!

Linnette always forgot her nine times tables. Oh rats, she thought, 9 x 9 = what? I remember now. The nine table always adds up to nine, up to 9 x 10. So, 9 x 1 = 9, 9 x 2 = 18 (because 1 + 8 = 9), 9 x 3 = 27, 9 x 4 = 36, 9 x 5= 45, 9 x 6 = 54, 9 x 7 = 63, 9 x 8 = 72, 9 x 9 = 81 because the answer, 81, when added together, 8 + 1 = 9. I got it!

Daniel was confident until it came to the following question: *Circle the correct spelling: separate, seperate, sepirate.* What did his mom say? "There's a rat in separate." Got it!

Name the months of the year that contain only 30 days, read Lance. What was that rhyme? Thirty days hath September, April, June, and November. All the rest have 31, except February, with 28. Well, it didn't exactly rhyme. Uh oh, the next one was tough. *When will the next leap year be?* Hmmmmmm! The United States elects presidents in leap years! That's it! Mrs. Dawes ended the test with a trick question. *Write the 50 states in 30 seconds.* The kids were stunned as she counted from 30 backwards. Only Daniel looked calm as he wrote quickly.

Ms. Dawes was so pleased that so many students got As. "How did you do it" she asked. My mother helped," said Daniel proudly. Ms. Dawes couldn't figure that one out. "But," she said, "Daniel was the only one who got the last question right. He knew the trick. Tell them, Daniel."

Daniel held up his paper. It said THE 50 STATES. Ms. Dawes laughed. "That one won't count," she said.

Name _____

Understanding and Enjoying What You Read

Answer the questions below. Reread the story if necessary.

1. Think of and write a trick to help you remember something important. _____

   _____

2. Write a different sentence to remember the order of the planets. _____

   _____

3. Finish the rhymes below to learn facts about history and science.

   Not even one man is now alive,
   Who saw the war against England in 177___.

   They landed on the moon and it was fine,
   In nineteen hundred and sixty-_____.

   It has no people, it has no cars.
   Our neighbor, the red planet, is known as _____.

4. Circle the best synonym (a word that means the same or nearly the same for another word) for *boast:*

   show off   brag   whine   tell

5. Do you think it was a good idea for Daniel to share what his mom taught him with his friends?
   Explain. _____

   _____

6. Testaphobia is a word that Brett's mother made up. Words ending in *phobia,* however, mean
   fear. Following are some common phobias: 1. xenophobia—fear of foreigners 2. acrophobia—
   fear of heights 3. agoraphobia—fear of the marketplace; It has also come to mean fear of
   leaving one's home. 4. arachnophobia—fear of spiders 5. claustrophobia—fear of confined
   quarters, such as an elevator or closet
   On the back of this page, write sentences using each of these words.

7. What might give you "schoolaphobia" for one day? _____

8. Name the planets in order, but backwards! Make up a sentence to help you remember them.

   _____

9. Look at these words: *believe, receive, reprieve.* Now, read the rule: I before E except after C.
   What does this old sentence help you remember? _____

   _____

10. Would you help your friends so they'd get good grades? Explain. _____

    _____

11. What do you think would have happened if Daniel hadn't known the tips? _____

    _____

Try This!   Write a rhyme to help someone remember your birthday!

The After-School Job

Name _____

Help Wanted. Excellent after-school job for hard-working boy or girl. Call 310-555-1234 and ask for Mrs. Kendrick.

Lance read the notice with excitement. He had wanted a new fishing rod ever since Uncle Roy and Aunt Isabel had taught him how to fish during the summer. They never ate the fish. They caught them and then gently removed the hook and let the fish swim away. Aunt Isabel said the pond on their property belonged to the fish, too. Uncle Roy thought it was silly to catch them and not eat them, but his wife insisted. When Lance had asked his mom and dad for a fishing rod, they had said, "Well, son, why don't you earn the money yourself? Money doesn't grow on trees, you know!"

Lance had tried to get some jobs around the neighborhood, but almost everyone had said, "You're too young, kid. Come back in a few years." He went home and called the number. A woman answered. She asked Lance a lot of questions. Did he like little ones? Did he like to play games with them? Would he feed her little one? Wow! thought Lance. This is a baby-sitting job. He said he'd be right there.

"Mom! Dad! I got a job. I'm baby-sitting for a little kid!" Lance's twin brother Bob came in. "You can't even take care of yourself. You need a babysitter!"

Mom said, "You're not even eleven, Lance. Meet with this nice woman, but tell her no. We're sorry."

Lance dragged himself to McDougall Street to a cozy old house with a large shade tree in the front. This was going to be embarrassing. He thought for sure he could take this job. He rang the doorbell. It played the song "Bingo." An elderly woman with a kind face and white hair answered. She was probably the grandma of the baby, Lance thought.

"Come in," she said warmly. Her voice was like sugary maple syrup. "I'm Mrs. Kendrick. The little darling is resting. You can see him, though." They tiptoed into a small room. Lance looked around. There, in a big straw basket, almost hidden on a soft, fluffy cushion, was a tiny dog with huge eyes. On the basket was a sign that said "Bingo."

"Here he is," said Mrs. Kendrick. "I need you to walk him every day, play with him—he has lots of toys—and talk to him. He's very intelligent, as you'll discover. I'll pay you four dollars an hour."

"I'll start now," said Lance. He put Bingo's leash on him and walked the tiny dog over to his own house. "Mom, Dad, Bob, I brought the baby home with me," he called.

As they rushed in, he heard his dad say, "We said no, Lance," then he stopped. Bingo jumped up, right into Dad's arms, and gave him a big, wet doggy kiss.

"Here's the baby," laughed Lance. "I'll have the money for that fishing rod soon."

Bob smiled at his brother and said, "Does his 'mother' have one I can sit for?"

FS-30024 Reading Comprehension

The After-School Job

Name _____

Understanding and Enjoying What You Read

Answer the questions below. Reread the story if necessary.

1. Did you think Lance's parents would let him keep the job? Explain. _____
_____

2. What would have happened if the dog had been a big, ferocious guard dog? _____
_____

3. Write the names of every kind of dog you know. Here's a start: poodle, German shepherd,
_____
_____
_____

4. If Lance couldn't baby-sit for Mrs. Kendrick, what should he have told her? _____
_____

5. Describe the place where Mrs. Kendrick lived. _____
_____

6. Why did Lance think he was going to sit for a baby? _____
_____

7. Why do you think Mrs. Kendrick needed someone to walk her dog? _____
_____

8. Why would Bob want to sit for a "baby" like Bingo? _____
_____

9. What kind of job would you want after school? _____

10. On the back of this page, write an ad to put in the paper advertising for a job for yourself. Don't forget to write the nicest things about yourself.

11. Write some good rules for taking care of Bingo. _____
_____
_____
_____

12. If Lance's fishing rod cost $52.00, how many hours would he have to work to earn it? _____

13. Why do you think people might not want to hire a boy Lance's age? _____
_____

14. Why did Lance think Mrs. Kendrick would be a baby's grandmother? _____
_____

15. Would you want Lance for a friend? Explain. _____
_____

Try This! Have a debate with a friend or friends about how old kids should be before they can baby-sit.

© Frank Schaffer Publications, Inc.   25   FS-30024 Reading Comprehension

The Big Race

Name _____

"There's going to be a race!" said Emily. "Everybody in the fifth and sixth grades gets to try out. No fifth-grader has ever won. The winner gets a big medal, like the ones they give in the Olympics, only not real gold."

"Brett will win," Daniel assured her. "He's the biggest, fastest, toughest guy at school. Nobody wants to run against him anyway."

"I do," they heard a soft voice say. They looked around. It was the brand-new student, Robert. He was skinny and small, about the same size as Lance.

"Look, you're new here," said Linnette. "You don't know how it works. Brett will beat you up if you even try, Robert."

"I'm not going to just try, I'm going to win. And call me Bo. All my friends call me Bo." With that, he hurled himself into the air and did four front flips in a row. Then he ran over to the basketball court to shoot a few baskets. He sank every one.

"Wow!" said David admiringly. "Maybe he has a chance. He looks like a good athlete."

"But shouldn't somebody discourage him? Brett hates to lose. And I hate to be around him when he does lose!"

The kids tried to persuade Bo not to run against Brett. Brett did, too. He glowered at Bo every chance he got. He tried to intimidate him all day, every day, every chance he got.

But Bo never gave up. He just tried to keep out of Brett's way.

Every day, Bo practiced running. The kids and Ms. Dawes helped him by timing him. Soon there was a regular Bo fan club. Brett came over.

"I guess you think he's going to beat me. He's a little shrimp. He can't beat me at anything. He'd better watch out. And everybody that helps him better watch out, too."

The day of the race approached. Bo was still in it. So were Brett and a couple of other boys and girls. Brett hadn't expected so many kids to run against him.

The whistle blew. Bo's skinny legs took off like a whirlwind. He left everybody in the dust right away. Near the finish line, he saw Brett huffing and puffing and gaining on him. The crowd of kids was yelling, "Go Bo!" over and over again. Not even feeling tired, Bo sped up and crossed the finish line with ease. Brett was second. Linnette was third.

Some of the kids hoisted Bo up on their shoulders. Others were quiet. Everybody waited to see what Brett was going to do. He came up to Bo.

"Well, I guess I'm the one who better watch out. High five, Bo." They slapped hands in the air and started walking away together. "Want to join our football team, Bo? I bet you're really good at that, too," Brett said, smiling.

"Boy, am I surprised!" said Linnette.

"Everybody is," said David. "And you're also the third place winner! Congratulations!"

The Big Race

Name _____

Understanding and Enjoying What You Read

Answer the questions below. Reread the story if necessary.

1. What did you expect Brett to do when Bo won? _____
   _____

2. Why did a little guy like Bo feel so good about himself? _____
   _____

3. Would you like to have a friend like Bo? Explain. _____
   _____

4. Why did more kids than expected race against Brett? _____
   _____

5. Explain the following: "Bo sped up and crossed the finish line *with ease.*" _____
   _____

6. Circle all the action verbs in the story. Action verbs tell what someone or something did. *Run, jump, speak*, and *blow* are all action verbs.

7. How do you know that Brett was getting tired during the race?_____
   _____

8. Why couldn't the winners get medals of real gold? _____
   _____

9. Why did the kids hoist Bo up on their shoulders? _____
   _____

10. Why was Brett such a bully? _____

11. How did the kids and Ms. Dawes help Bo? _____
    _____

12. Match the words with the closest meaning by writing the number next to it.

    1. intimidate   2. discourage   3. persuade   4. whirlwind   5. hoist

    _____ to convince   _____ to lift or haul up   _____ to make less hopeful
    _____ to frighten by threats   _____ a current of air that rotates rapidly

13. What things did Brett do to intimidate people so they wouldn't run against him? _____
    _____

14. Why was Brett smart to make friends with Bo at the end? _____
    _____

15. Linnette was the third place winner. How come she didn't make a fuss about it? _____
    _____

Try This! Write a different ending for this story.

FS-30024 Reading Comprehension

The Country Report

Name _____

Ms. Dawes' class had been waiting for this all year—the country reports.

"Everyone has to choose a country to do a report on," said Ms. Dawes. "Call consulates, visit travel agencies, go to the library. I want interesting reports from everyone."

"What country are you going to choose?" Emily asked David.

"Wyoming," he answered.

"That's not a country, it's a state," she informed him.

"Do you think Ms. Dawes will notice?" he asked. "Then I'll take France. How about you?"

Suddenly, Brett broke in. "I'm taking Andorra," he said. "It's a tiny country near France that lots of people have never even heard of. I bet Ms. Dawes has never heard of it either. There's hardly any information about it, so my report can be real, real short, and it won't be my fault!"

"You're just lazy," said Linnette. "I'm doing Germany. There's lots of information about it, and I have some artifacts from it and everything. I know I'll get an A."

"What's an artifact?" asked Brett.

"It's something from a place, like those arrowheads you brought to school. Those are Indian artifacts. They tell something about people."

"Hey!" said Brett. "I have artifacts—my baseball cards. In a million years, when they dig them up, they'll know about me!"

"Yeah, you'll go down in history as the boy who did an Andorra report."

"I was opening the closet door, and the C volume of the encyclopedia fell on my head," said Emily. "So I'm taking Colombia. It's named after Christopher Columbus, you know."

"Why?" asked David. He was getting curious about this country.

"On his last voyage to America, Columbus sailed near Colombia, so they named it after him. But he wasn't actually the first European who explored it."

"Tell me more," said David. "Maybe it'll make me want to start my report."

Emily continued. "Well, the Spanish started exploring Colombia in the sixteenth century. They had heard of an Indian chieftain who covered himself in powdered gold. They called him El Dorado, which means *The Gilded One*, in Spanish. They looked all over the place and never found him. But they built settlements. Pretty soon, Spain had taken over most of South America, except for that huge country Brazil, which the Portuguese took. A lot of Indians were killed. They didn't want to be taken over. Nowadays, Spanish is still the official language, and they sell a lot of coffee. They have gold—the legend was right about that—and also coal, iron, and emeralds which are precious green stones. The capital is Bogotá. Colombia is a republic. Most of the people are farmers, although many live in the cities, too. Children have to go to school from age seven to eleven. Colombia is the only South American country that has a coastline that faces both the Caribbean Sea and the Pacific Ocean. I'd like to visit Colombia someday."

"Me, too," said David. "Maybe our class can go there on a field trip. It's only a few thousand miles away!"

FS-30024 Reading Comprehension

The Country Report

Understanding and Enjoying What You Read

Answer the questions below. Reread the story if necessary.

1. What is unusual about the coastline of Colombia? _____
   _____
   _____

2. Who was in Colombia before the Spanish? _____

3. What is the official language of Colombia? _____

4. How many years must Colombian children attend school? _____

5. What is the precious stone found in Colombia? _____

6. Why do you think people value gold so much? _____
   _____

7. Why couldn't the class really go to Colombia on a field trip? _____

8. Why did Emily choose Colombia for her report? _____
   _____

9. Write five words that you think describe Colombia. _____
   _____

10. What do you think of Brett's character? _____
    _____

11. What's the difference between a state and a country? _____
    _____

12. Make a list of artifacts that would tell people of the future about you. _____
    _____
    _____
    _____
    _____

13. Compare Emily and Brett as students. _____
    _____
    _____

14. What would you like to do to go down in history? _____
    _____
    _____
    _____

Try This! Close your eyes and choose a volume of the encyclopedia. Choose a country in that volume, and write a report on it.

Name _____

Snodgrass fifth grade was on their way to Camp Conrad for science camp. When they got to the camp, the kids did arts and crafts, made bird feeders for the many noisy birds they heard, and hiked.

"I'm hungry as a bear," said Lance.

"Speaking of bears, I hope we don't see any," worried Daniel.

"Snakes! I don't want to see any of those slithery, slimy snakes," said Emily. She shuddered just thinking about them. Suddenly, she saw Mr. Giles, one of the cabin leaders, walking toward her with a gigantic snake!

"Eeek!" Emily yelled. "I knew these woods were dangerous!"

Mr. Giles backed off and said, "I'm sorry you're scared, Emily. This is Natasha. I didn't find her in the woods. She lives with me. She's a boa constrictor. Come on, pet her." Emily just froze where she was.

"I'll pet her, Mr. Giles," said David. "Hey! She's not slimy! She's smooth and kind of warm. Try it, Emily."

But Emily would have no part of the long snake.

That night, there was a big campfire. Afterwards, the girls went back to the cabin. Their cabin leader, Ms. Dawes, told them a scary story. Then she went to visit with the other teachers.

"I wish Ms. Dawes hadn't left us alone," shivered Linnette. Just then, the door opened with a squeak.

"It—it's a bear," whispered Linnette. "Don't anybody move." The bear growled. It held out a furry paw and touched Emily. She reached down, got out her hair dryer, and whacked the bear over the head. It roared and left. When Ms. Dawes heard the story, she couldn't believe it!

The next morning, David showed up at breakfast but Daniel was absent. "Where's Daniel?" the girls asked.

"Well, he has a bad headache today. He. . .uh fell out of his bunk and has a big bump on his head."

Emily laughed. "Tell him, we hope he can BEAR it!"

Understanding and Enjoying What You Read

Answer the questions. Reread the story if necessary.

1. Check the main idea of the story.
   _____ Fifth-graders went to camp and were visited by a bear.
   _____ Kids went on a hike.   _____ A girl knocked a bear on the head.
   _____ Camp was full of animals.   _____ Boys were not going to behave.

Answer the questions below on the back of this paper.

2. What does the ending of the story mean?

3. What would have happened if a real bear had been in the cabin?

4. Do you think Emily will pet Natasha the snake before science camp is over? Explain.

5. Write a list of all the animals listed in the story. Then write a list of forest animals that could have been included.

6. How did the girls know that Daniel was the bear?

7. Pretend your class is going to camp. Write what you would like to do, what you might be afraid of, and who your friends would be.

Answers

Page 3
1. Kids decide to solve a case.
2.-5. Answers will vary.
6. 1, 3, 4, 2
7. Answers will vary.
8. basic, introductory, simple
9. Answers will vary.
10. A phenomenon in space that contains a heavy field of gravity. It may be a collapsed star; things can get stuck in it.
11. Answers will vary.
12. Answers may vary.—angry; Emily tapped her foot to show impatience.
13. Answers will vary.
14. Emily suggests that they work together from now on.

Page 5
1. Emily and David try to trick Daniel.
2. Answers may vary.—She could have kept the money.
3. Answers may vary.—Daniel is her friend.
4. Answers will vary.
5. a. F, b. T, c. F, d. T
6. 1—imagine, 3—an agreement, 2—to fool, 10—not generous, 5—combined; as one, 6—a penalty, 9—fake, 4—getting even, 7—shock, 8—to make known, 11—honestly
7. Check students' stories.
8. Answers may vary.—She was embarrassed.
9. Answers will vary.
10. Answers may vary.—She was trying to show him it was a joke.
11. Answers may vary.—He was being a pest.

Page 7
1. Lance and Bob are identical twins who don't look alike.
2.-3. Answers will vary.

4. 2, 4, 3, 1, 5
5. Answers may vary.—Accept anything in pairs.
6.-10. Answers will vary.
11. Bob—tall, wide face, 10 pounds heavier than Lance: Lance—short, narrow face, thin
12. Answers will vary.
13. wide—narrow, apart—together, friends—enemies, wrong—right
14. Check students' stories.

Page 9
1. Emily is worried about sharing her birthday.
2. Answers will vary.
3. F, T, F, T, T
4.-9. Answers will vary.
10. Answers may vary.—They would fill the holes with melted wax.
11. Answers may vary.—He doesn't like to try new things.
12. Check students' stories.
13. Answers will vary.
14. Answers may vary.—Emily was too concerned about sharing her birthday with George Washington.

Page 11
1. The class went on a game show to win a trophy.
2. Linnette; The theory of relativity, $E=mc^2$; He helped the United States build the first atomic bomb.
3. Answers may vary.—She admired him.
4. Answers will vary depending on the year.
5. Answers may vary.—She might have gotten stage fright. A trance is a dazed or dreamy condition.

6. Answers may vary.—He was obnoxious.
7.-9. Answers will vary.
10. a. obnoxious, b. paused, c. genius, d. science

Page 13
1. Emily takes her friends to her new house.
2.-3. Answers will vary.
4. the storm, lightning
5. 4, 5, 3, 1, 2
6. Answers will vary.
7. Answers may vary.—terrified, frightened, spooky
8.-10. Answers will vary.
11. twilight
12. Answers may vary.—because they bought a spooky house
13. Answers will vary.
14. Answers may vary.—It's a "bad luck" day. Lots of things could happen.
15. death

Page 15
1. Emily goes shopping for her birthday party and wins free food.
2. Answers may vary.—so she'll have a great party
3. Answers will vary.
4. Check students' stories.
5. Answers may vary.—cake, ice cream, sandwiches
6. Answers will vary.
7. 451, 555, **682**
8. Answers will vary.
9. candy, soda, paper goods, bakery, pet food, fancy food
10. peanuts, lemon cake, chocolate, coconut, spinach
11.-14. Answers will vary.
15. aisle—a passageway between rows of seats; isle—an island, especially a small one

Page 17

1. Three friends have a fun day at the beach.
2. Answers will vary.
3. Answers may vary.—We would have more skin cancer.
4.-5. Answers will vary.
6. at dinnertime
7. an ichthyologist
8. His skin was darker.
9. Their skin is lighter.
10.-12. Answers will vary.
13. Check students' stories.
14. Answers will vary.

Page 19

1. A substitute teaches a class a lesson.
2. Answers will vary.—Definition: To trick, to deceive by trickery
3.-4. Answers will vary.
5. Check students' stories.
6. Answers may vary.—squeaked, mentioned, moaned, suggested
7.-9. Answers will vary.
10. Answers may vary.—She knew what the kids were up to.
11. "It's what kids do," said Daniel.
12. Answers may vary.—He's going crazy.
13. Answers will vary.
14. 3
15. Answers will vary.

Page 21

1. Kids go to Bob and Lance's birthday party and participate in a scavenger hunt.
2. 5, 3, 2, 4, 1
3. Check students' stories.
4. Answers will vary.
5. Answers may vary.—teamwork

6.-8. Answers will vary.
9. a safety pin, a quarter, a lottery ticket, friends; Answers will vary.
10. A cockatiel is a small, parrotlike bird from Australia.
11.-12. Answers will vary.
13. Answers may vary.—They looked through it thoroughly.

Page 23

1.-2. Answers will vary.
3. 5, nine, Mars
4. brag
5.-6. Answers will vary.
7. Answers may vary.—a test
8. Pluto, Neptune, Uranus, Saturn, Jupiter, Mars, Earth, Venus, Mercury
9. Whether e or i comes first in a word
10.-11. Answers will vary.

Page 25

1.-4. Answers will vary.
5. It was a cozy old house with a large shade tree in front.
6. Answers may vary.—The lady described what sounded like a baby.
7. Answers will vary.
8. Answers may vary.—Bingo is a friendly, nice dog.
9.-11. Answers will vary.
12. 13
13. Answers will vary.
14. Answers may vary.—She was old.
15. Answers will vary.

Page 27

1.-4. Answers will vary.
5. It was easy for him to do.
6. Check students' stories.
7. He was huffing and puffing.

8. Answers may vary.—They would be too expensive.
9. Answers may vary.—He won and they like him. He stood up to Brett.
10. Answers will vary.
11. They helped him practice.
12. 3—to convince, 4—a current of air that rotates rapidly, 1—to frighten by threats, 5—to lift or haul up, 2—to make less hopeful
13. He said they'd better watch out.
14.-15. Answers will vary.

Page 29

1. The coastline faces both the Caribbean Sea and the Pacific Ocean.
2. the Indians
3. Spanish
4. 4
5. emeralds
6. Answers will vary.
7. It's too far.
8. The C volume of the encyclopedia fell on her head.
9. Answers may vary.—republic, gold, emeralds, resources
10. Answers may vary.—He's lazy.
11. A state is an area within a country.
12.-14. Answers will vary.

Page 30

1. Fifth-graders went to camp and were visited by a bear.
2. Answers may vary.—The word *bear* has several meanings. It can refer to the animal, or it can mean *to endure*.
3.-7. Answers will vary.